PORSCHE 968

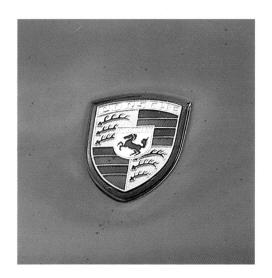

PORSCHE 968

David Sparrow and
Adrienne Kessel

This book is dedicated to Matthew Ward

First published in Great Britain in 1994
by Osprey, an imprint of Reed Consumer
Books Limited, Michelin House,
81 Fulham Road, London SW3 6RB and
Auckland, Melbourne, Singapore and Toronto.

ISBN 1 85532 437 7

Editor Nicolas Caldon
Page design Paul Kime/Ward Peacock
Partnership

Printed in Hong Kong

Produced by Mandarin Offset

Acknowledgements

Our heartfelt thanks go to the following:
Claire Knee and John Edwards of Porsche Cars Great Britain; Udo
Lahm, Susan Hutter, Eberhard Scholl, Bernd Oergel, Klaus Parr and
Peter Schnieder at Zuffenhausen; Thomas Herold and Klaus
Steckkonig at Weissach; Petra Eckhardt of Porsche Austria GmbH;
Michael Ticehurst, specialist 924 dealer of Henley-on-Thames; Ian
Anderson for translating original material; models Sandra Kauelly and
Jade Bond and 'Miss Selfridge' for Miss Bond's clothes.

The photographs in this book were all taken with Leica R6 cameras
and Leica lenses. Film used was exclusively Kodachrome 64 and 200
ISO – both in the amateur stock as David Sparrow finds that this
stands up better to non-refrigerated travel!

Front cover
*In the late sixties Ferry Porsche said of
his cars 'what is important is to do them
well.' Twenty-five years on 968 lives up
to that maxim*

Back cover
*Porsche claim a commitment to the
building of sports cars – but sports cars
that can be driven as day to day
transport . The expertise and knowledge
that they gain through intensive tests like
the 100,000Km run is invaluable and
reflected in the development and
refinement of cars that can find
themselves in a variety of day-to-day
conditions*

Half-title page
*For sheer motoring enjoyment there is no
better guarantee than the Porsche badge*

Title page
*Instantly recognisable as one of the
Porsche family, the 968's sleek lines are
a joy to behold in any setting*

For a catalogue of all books published by Osprey Automotive
please write to:

**The Marketing Department, Reed Consumer Books,
1st Floor, Michelin House, 81 Fulham Road, London SW3 6RB**

The fruit of all that behind-the-scenes effort and skill — a star takes centre stage

Contents

Despite the abundance of automation and technology, there are some jobs that can only be done by a trained hand and eye. Porsche are justifiably proud of their paint finish; the fine polishing which prepares the surface for its paint coats is one of the jobs where man surpasses machine

'At Porsche we only build sports cars.'

Ferdinand Alexander Porsche's proud maxim sums up the marque's tradition of producing classic vehicles for both the race and road worlds. The new 968 looks set to continue that tradition with a combination of style, value and performance that is hard to match in a market bulging with similarly priced coupés.

The philosophy and developmental ability that Porsche have brought to bear on the 968 have their roots in the company's earliest days when 'Dr. Ing. h.c.F. Porsche KG Design Office for Engines and Vehicles' was set up by Ferdinand Porsche in 1931 in Stuttgart to provide quality design and development skills to the rapidly expanding German car industry. By 1940, his Stuttgart-based venture had undertaken no less than 104 projects. Major milestones included the design of the Auto Union racing car type 22, the first car that successfully used modern, mid-engine construction, and the 'Volkswagen' or 'people's car' that was to become the ubiquitous and much loved Beetle. The first car to bear the Porsche name was the 356. Powered by a modified air-cooled VW engine the 356 was available in both Cabriolet and Coupé versions, although in limited numbers as it was hand built. Production began in earnest in 1950 at the Reutter factory next door to Porsche at Zuffenhausen. When the model celebrated its tenth birthday, more than 25,000 had been sold world-wide.

Ferdinand Porsche died in 1951, and the company came under the control of his son, Ferry. In the late sixties, he realised that Porsche needed to broaden their model range in the direction of a more affordable sports car. Introduced in 1964 the 911, with its rear-mounted six cylinder engine, was popular, although its high cost was restricting the joys of Porsche-ownership to those with the money to afford it. A partner was needed with experience of volume production; VW, with whom Porsche already shared a working relationship, were the obvious

The rounded shapes and unbroken lines of the 356 are reminders of its VW Beetle ancestry. The slope of the wings and curve of the headlights have once again found favour; 968, while most definitely a 90's shape, has a strong family resemblance to its forbears

Above

At first glance, the front of a 914 with headlights closed looks more like the back of a car. This is especially true of the American version, with completely amber side lights and large reflectors on the wing. The shape of the front was roundly criticised by purists for being too un-Porsche

Right

The 928 would become Porsche's top-of-the-range car and was already being planned and developed at Weissach when VW approached them to design their new sports car. However, it would not be launched until the spring of 1977, over a year after the 924

choice. The product of this union was the mid-engined VW-Porsche type 914. Unfortunately, management changes at VW resulted in loss of interest in the project. Porsche were conscious of a 'not-a-real-Porsche' attitude from some champions of the marque; they tried a completely Porsche-built version, the 914/6, powered by the 911 engine – but this made it more expensive, which defeated the original idea, and it never sold well.

By 1970 work was well underway at the new Porsche Development Centre in Weissach. Situated to the north-west of Stuttgart, Weissach then, as today, was expected to be self supporting. It was at this time that Volkswagen approached Porsche, although not for a joint venture. They wanted Porsche to design and develop a car that they would sell as

Above

'Functional design through aerodynamics, safety, corrosion resistance, reparability, economic production and operation – such are the critical points to be observed during today's body development.'

(From a paper on the main development objectives of the 924 body, by Hermann E. Burst ans Rainer Srock of the Research and Development Centre, Weissach)

Left

Thirty years of automotive expertise for hire. Porsche's new development facilities, sports car orientation plus the bonus of a previous working relationship made them the obvious choice for VW. This rare photograph from the Porsche archives shows a model of the VW-badged car that was to become the 924

a VW. A front-engine design that owed some aspects of its styling to the 928, already in the process of development at Weissach, was chosen. The car would be powered by a water-cooled Audi engine, later used in the Audi 100.

The best laid plans go awry. 1973 saw the car market generally, and sports cars in particular, suffering from the aftermath of the oil crisis. Again, management changes at VW heralded a change of direction; the project, as far as VW were concerned, was scuppered. Porsche were reluctant to wave good-bye to the idea as money had been spent, and expertise gained; valuable commodities that were not to be wasted. Porsche bought the project from VW and put more money into bringing it through development and into production.

This move brought the 924 into being. As was originally intended, it was built at the Audi plant in Neckarsulm, thus utilising Audi's spare production capability. The 1984 cc engine was a single-overhead camshaft four, which delivered 125 bhp. The engine was front-mounted, driving the rear wheels. However, research at Weissach during 928 development has indicated the unmistakable benefits of siting the gearbox over the driving wheels in the form of a transaxle – a solution that achieved near perfect weight distribution. The lines of the 924 were designed to be smooth and unobtrusive. Retractable head lamps, rounded bumpers, shielded windscreen wipers and flush rear lights were preferred – not just for aerodynamic reasons but also for safety. Pillars need to be as narrow as possible for visibility, but substantial enough to be strong, affording maximum protection of passengers in the event of an accident.

With the introduction of the 924 Turbo, Porsche took a small step towards the goal of completely in-house production; engines were brought the short distance to Zuffenhausen from Neckarsulm, and all the turbocharging and assembly stages took place under the Porsche roof.

In the late seventies, it became clear that Porsche would have to find an alternative engine for the 924, or the car that was heavily rumoured to be its replacement. Audi had stopped producing the original engine for its own purposes; there were many Porsche aficionados who felt that the whole concept was not quite Porsche enough – and Porsche themselves wished to continue the trend of the 924 Turbo.

The new 944 was introduced to its public at the Frankfurt Motor Show in 1981. It was built around the basic chassis of its predecessor the 924, with the same transaxle arrangement. Some components were taken from the Turbo version. The 2479 cc engine, based on that of its bigger brother the 928 – on half of its V8 to be precise, delivered 163 bhp. There were no radical new styling departures for the 944. It was slightly fuller to look at, especially at the sides, which made it appear lower and more road-hugging than 924.

1985 saw the introduction of the 944 Turbo, a model that owed much to the racing heritage of Porsche. Emission figures and abilities with unleaded fuel were now part of the design equation for all manufacturers. One of Porsche's aims was to ensure that performance continued to be maximised, whether or not a catalytic converter was fitted. The third car in the 944 range was the 944S; its sixteen valve engine produced 190 bhp, compared with the 220 bhp of its turbocharged stablemate.

The turbocharged engine, which gave 170bhp, required style changes at the front end; air intakes appeared on the nose, with an air duct breaking the line of the bonnet

Above

Although the 'not-Porsche-enough' tag still stuck to the 924 in some more die-hard quarters on account of its water-cooled 1984cc four-cylinder engine, there were many who preferred its styling to that of the 944

Right

The 944 styling at launch. Although it had a slightly altered lighting arrangement the 944 basically had the same front shape as 924

Much as the original 944 was developed around its predecessor, the 924, so the 968 owes much of its heritage to the 944. While the chassis and basic dimensions remain similar, it is the styling and mechanical changes that makes the differences clear. From Tiptronic transmission to the highest torque of any normal 3.0 litre engine in series production, the 968 may well, as Ferdinand Alexander Porsche points out: 'represent a new chapter in the history of the sports car.'

Above
The distinctive 944 shape; while the exterior dimensions were virtually the same as for the 924 its more bulbous contours made it look lower and longer

Above right
With the introduction of the 944 Turbo, front styling changed to incorporate a skirt with intake bands. The lighting configuration changed too

Right
Porsche have usually incorporated an 'S' version into their plans and thus the 944S completed the range. The 944S 2 had Turbo styling, which included a rear extractor skirt in body colour

Overleaf
Time marches on; 944 was the standard bearer for the lowest-priced model range for a decade. Along with the 911 and 928 it formed a successful and sustained three-pronged attack on the sports car market

Looking back over its shoulder to Audi days? Maybe, but the car destined to carry the Porsche flag against stiff competition from the VW Corrado VR6, Mazda RX7 and Renault Alpine A610 is an all new car with a new number on its tail – 968

Weissach

In the late 1960s, Professor Ferry Porsche conceived and developed a remarkable new project – the Porsche Development Centre in Weissach. The centre co-ordinates all Porsche research and development projects, employing over 25 per cent of the company's workforce and utilising over 16 acres of workshops and offices, plus three race tracks. The Centre is important to the local community as well; so much so that the main street proudly bears the name 'Porschestrasse! It is here that Porsche take design projects right through to the production stage, and where the 968 was born.

Not all the work done at Weissach is for Porsche's sole benefit; over forty per cent of the research work is done for external clients, be they other manufacturers or other Governments. The work is not just automotive; it was here that the Leopard tank was originated and the decision taken to power the Skyship 500 with engines from the 911 Series!

As safety needs and environmental awareness have increased, so the Weissach technology has expanded to suit. Porsche is one of a number of European car manufacturers working on the PROMETHEUS research project, which aims to find balanced solutions to problems of traffic flow, environmental damage, safety and economy.

As a self-contained operation, the work at the Development Centre is based on the principle that a project team supplies all the information and know-how for every aspect of a vehicle's design and development; and that, by having all the necessary facilities in one place, simultaneous research and development processes compliment each other.

Those processes are mind-bogglingly varied. In the workshops there are departments dealing with machining, plastics-processing, assembly and painting to name but a few. Everything is covered, from engine test rigs and air and liquid flow labs to roller dynamometers, flywheel test rigs and acoustic measuring chambers. Most spectacular and the full- and quarter-scale wind tunnels, climatic chambers and full crash testing facilities.

Porsche claim that the Development Centre will never be complete; it is an on-going project that will always need be ready to adapt to changes in technology, in expectations, in the world in general.

Thus Porsche's methods of design and development at Weissach are geared towards a totally harmonious end product; body styling, engine

The Weissach Development Centre is surrounded by beautiful rolling countryside, 30 minutes drive from the Porsche factory at Zuffenhausen. Its state-of-the-art facilities are constantly reviewed and improved to ensure Porsche's position at the forefront of motoring development and design

The Centre's buildings are modern, with a calm but confident businesslike air. Within this high-tech environment, teams of engineers, stylists, technicians and scientists work on projects for clients around the world – as well as pushing forward Porsche's own development aims

and gearbox development, chassis configuration, safety considerations, all must come together to create a vehicle that is more than the sum of its component parts. It is for this reason that each project is handled by a closely knit team – each member an expert in his or her particular field. Everyone within the team must also have an overview of the car that appreciates the ways in which the various disciplines inter-react; from this mix comes the car's individual personality.

Despite such individuality, the team at Weissach retained some of the classic Porsche design characteristics on the 968 with the rounded headlamps and raked bonnet. It is under that bonnet where the more important changes appear.

The 3-litre, 16-valve engine produces 240 bhp and is one of the most powerful normally aspirated production engines in the world. It can take the car to 62.5 mph (100 km/h) in 6.5 seconds and, perhaps more

Above

Proving a point…or twenty. The Centre's proving ground replicates every type of surface that a tyre, suspension or braking system is ever likely to encounter. Continuous driving tests making use of the track's varied conditions can simulate many more miles of normal road driving

Right

Endurance tests are also carried out on public roads and at other racing or test tracks with different characteristics, such as the Nürburgring and Nardo in Italy

importantly, gives 200 Nm of torque at 1000 rpm, up to a maximum of 305 Nm at 4100 rpm. Such a high torque capability is in part down to Porsche's Variocam, an electronically controlled variable camshaft timing system which improves torque by varying the timing of the inlet camshaft in relation to the exhaust camshaft. The system also improves exhaust gas quality, complementing the 3-way metallic exhaust gas catalytic converter (Porsche was the first manufacturer to offer its entire model range with a catalytic converter fitted as standard). Who says sports cars can't be environmentally friendly?

Porsche's attempts to satisfy environmental considerations are matched by the value the company places on safety. ABS brakes may be available on any number of cars these days, but Porsche were the first to make them standard across their whole range. The braking system is servo-assisted with four-piston fixed light alloy callipers and huge

internally ventilated discs. There are no problems stopping the **968** in its tracks. Add to that improved crumple zones incorporated into the bodywork, side intrusion bars, crush tubes and a roll-cage developed out of the roof, door frames and windscreen pillars; and what you have is an incredibly safe ride. All it needs is the airbag, currently fitted as standard in Germany, to be made available in the UK.

All this weight is distributed evenly between the front and rear of the car, as perfectly as it is possible to get, thanks to Porsche's transaxle driveline system. The driveshaft, protected within a strengthened steel tube, connects the front-mounted engine to the rear-mounted gearbox. The results, aided by a low center of gravity, are great handling and steering characteristics, which again add to the overall safety of the **968**.

There are two choices of transmission available with the **968**. The 6-speed manual gearbox has been newly designed with both performance and economy in mind. When the car has reached **62.5** mph in **6.5** seconds it is still in second gear! Fully loaded, gear changes will normally take place at more than **6000** rpm, the maximum rev limit being **6700** rpm. Gears one to five are the major players on public roads – number

six enables the cars to reach its maximum speed of 156 mph. At a constant speed of 56 mph however, an amazing fuel consumption figure of 39.2 mpg is within the bounds of possibility. This is indeed an engine that can be revved freely, and yet remains smooth and progressive right to the red line (when the governor cuts in). But what does amaze and delight is the degree of low-end torque. Sixth gear is quite usable at 70 mph, at which speed the 928 is simply ticking over. For added go whenovertaking, it will be judicious to swap some cogs, but on a motorway this will be mainly for the pleasure of producing a perfectly timed downward change, and that rewarding surge forward. This is a car that wants to be driven well.

The second transmission option is one of those rare solutions to any problem; a compromise that delivers the very best of both worlds. Porsche's Tiptronic system combines the advantages of an automatic

Above
In addition, the circuit incorporates specialised areas for testing specific functions; rubber on the skid pad indicates testing to the absolute limit, but in complete safety

Right
Alternate raises and dips are set to put the wheels diametrically off level. The 968 remained calm and unruffled, balanced from without and comfortable from within

Above

The benefits of teamwork. Here a 968 is put through its paces on the skid pad by Thomas Herold, one of the Project Management Team who has worked on the car from its conception right through the research, development and launch phases. He is still involved in the process of continuous improvement which goes on to the present day

Right

The village of Weissach has grown as with the expansion of the Porsche facility. A large proportion of the population work there. Much local business is connected directly or indirectly to the company or to its employees...hardly surprising then that the main street of Weissach is named Porschestrasse

gearbox with those of a manual one. When set in automatic mode, during stop/start town motoring for example, electronic sensors monitor the speed, accelerator position and direction of movement of the car, and select one of five settings accordingly. This monitoring effectively eliminates the disturbing effects which can reduce legs to jelly – such as the sudden unexpected surge that would otherwise occur when the accelerator is near to the floor or a sudden gearchange when braking in an emergency. A driver-induced increase in the rate of acceleration results in the most sporting setting being chosen – once the car slows again, the original setting is resumed. The manual setting is reached horizontally from the 'D' automatic position, and comprises a

Above
The winds of change are produced artificially here, and provide a splendid display of aerodynamics when combined with a 968 Coupé and a smoke stream

Above right
The wind tunnel at Weissach is always in great demand, whether from Porsche project teams or other customers. The latter are not always automotive, one of the more unusual guests being the football that was used in the 1992 European championships in Sweden

Right
Measurement is ultra-precise; the floor is marked and scaled for pinpoint accuracy. In another part of the building, a quarter-scale working model of the tunnel, first used to check the viability of the real thing prior to construction, is now used with proportionally scaled models for research purposes. The latest in technology fills the observation room along one side of the tunnel. Computer modelling, say the experts, has speeded and simplified the basics of aerodynamics in design. But to refine it, to get everything just right, they stress, takes something more besides; the instincts of an expert's mind. Teamwork once again; but this time man and machine

Above

*As the 924 and 944 amply proved, Porsche's transaxle driveline system achieves a
distribution of weight between the front and rear of the car which is as near perfect as
it is possible to get. The driveshaft, protected within a strengthened steel tube,
connects the front-mounted engine to the rear-mounted gearbox. Together with a low
centre of gravity, the even weighting results in excellent steering and handling of
unsurpassed neutrality*

Right

From the outside, the engine compartment of the car looks compact and unassuming

Left

Lift the cover and everything is neat and orderly; black finish pipes and cables, bright yellow caps to the oil filler and dipstick. Dominating the engine compartment, its smooth textured aluminium finish embossed with the Porsche logo, is the powerful 3-litre 16 valve engine which produces 240bhp

Above

The power from this engine is maximised by a unique feature – Porsche's Variocam, an electronically controlled camshaft timing system. It increases the engine output and the torque by varying the timing of the inlet camshaft in relation to the exhaust camshaft to increase the overlap. The system not only improves power and torque (by up to 5bph and 6lb ft respectively), it also improves the quality of the exhaust gases by substantially cutting the hydrocarbon emissions

Above

A sports car, but not a thirsty car – normal urban cycle consumption is around 32mpg

Left

Reached from the 'D' automatic position, the manual shift comprises a simple plus and minus selector

Overleaf

The environmental aspect of design has always been important to Porsche; car buyers have become more ecologically aware and a 'sports car' tag is no longer reason enough to pollute the atmosphere or run inefficiently. Porsche was among the first to fit catalytic converters to their cars as standard; the 968 is fitted with a controlled 3-way metallic exhaust gas converter, which is efficient enough to meet the legal requirements of any country in the world

simple plus and minus selector. This achieves upward and downward gear changes without the need for a clutch, simply with the touch of a selector. An indicator in the rev counter dial displays the current settings. The Coupe with Tiptronic reaches 62.5mph in 7.9 seconds, only 1.5 seconds slower than with the six-speed manual gearbox.

Above

When it does need filling up, the 968 runs on unleaded fuel.
A rubber flap reminds you to check the oil, though a decent interval should be left to
allow the oil to settle, and so avoid overfilling, with the possibility of blowing an oil seal

Left

As the volume of cars on the roads has increased, so has the need for a higher level of
safety, both active and passive. The greater the performance and speed capabilities of
the car, the larger the safety responsibilities become. Naturally, ABS anti-lock brakes
are fitted to the 968 as standard; together with a sophisticated power-assisted steering
system, they ensure that safe control is possible under all conditions

Left
The 968 was first presented during the summer of 1991, and was in production at Zuffenhausen by the autumn.
It has a clear identity; its lines confirm it as a newly styled design, but the 944 and 924 influences are obvious. Indeed, the doors, roof and hatch are all from 944, as are the rear wings, only slightly changed towards the rear to incorporate the brand new rear bumper, formed in the manner of the 928

Above
The 'original' Porsche shape, courtesy of its Volkswagen Beetle and 356 ancestors, is epitomised in the 911. This is the shape that says Porsche loud and clear; even to those without first hand knowledge of the marque. The distinctive rounded wings end in vertical headlamps while the smoothly curved bonnet carries the distinctive Porsche badge in the centre. Most important from a stylistic point of view, is the fact that 911 is recognisable by the way the front wings sit higher than the bonnet line

Above

968's wings are slightly rounded, extending forward of the bonnet front line and towards the centre. All the curves are subtle; they imply the shape of the 911 rather than copying it

Left

924 and 944 departed from this tradition; their lines were flatter and more square, with no rounding to the wings. The headlamps hid behind squared-off panels, the mirrors echoed their shape. Many customers preferred the less bulbous 924 to the 944

Above

When they are not in use the headlights are uncovered; their lines follow the curve of the wings and lie flush within them. When sidelights only are switched on, the light units remain in this position. Pop-up units were chosen not, as has been reported, to achieve a 928 look-alike, but to maintain the 911/959 heritage. To quote Harm Lagaay again 'At the time of development, it was not possible to achieve the optical performance without pop-up lights. Headlight development is continuing, and the course we have chosen will become clear with future models.' Watch out for the new shape 911!

Right

The halogen headlamps are newly designed with variable focus reflector system greatly increasing the light output. Foglamps which double as daylight driving lights are integrated into the front bumper section, along with the indicators. The top of the radiator aperture forms a straight line with the tops of these two lamp clusters

Above

When they are needed, the headlamps unfold to vertical. A safety device fitted to the folding mechanism ensures that no damage takes place if it should become fouled by some obstruction. Powerful washer jets keep the headlights free of road dirt

Left

Sports cars need good night-time illumination; the faster a car can be driven, the more important it is to be able to see the road ahead with clarity and accuracy. The 968 headlamps provide superb night vision which inspires confidence even when driving on winding tree lined country lanes

Above
The Coupé's fixed spoiler aids its aerodynamic styling; extensive tests have proved that this automobile has one of the lowest drag figures of any car, anywhere

Left
Distinctive rear light clusters in the unlit state appear completely red; special optics and coloured filters enable their horizontal divisions to show white reversing lights and orange indicators too

Back to the 911 for the origins of the side spoiler shape. Stone chip protection is provided by a plastic coating which rises above the spoiler at the wheel arch

The 944 incorporated stone-chip protection in a similar line from door to wheel arch along its spoilerless rear panel

Above

Another family likeness; all three models now have their number designations, in familiar Porsche digits, centrally placed at the rear

Left

Front and rear sections are manufactured from impact absorbing polyurethane material. These withstand impacts of up to five kilometres per hour, thus reducing the chances of damage from the minor impacts that are an inevitable part of day-to-day motoring

Above

968 takes this one stage further. Its side spoilers are a clear design element. Their shape improves aerodynamics while they have the stone guards integrated into them

Right

The 968 is fitted with 16 inch cup design light alloy wheels, fitted with either Pirelli or Michelin low profile tyres. The large openings of these wheels ensures excellent brake cooling. When the uprated sports suspension package is fitted, the car comes with 17 inch Bridgestones

Above

A feature of the 968 wheel is the asymmetric rim, which prevents the tyre slipping or coming away in the event of a puncture. It is thus possible to drive slowly on to the next convenient place for tyre changing or repair

Right

Wherever it goes, the Porsche exterior says style. Whether or not one is familiar with the details of its design – the subtle curve of the front wing, the continuing line of the spoilers from side to rear – that family likeness is clear. Wherever it goes, 968 will be a crowd-puller

Above

Weather that cannot be relied upon is not a uniquely English phenomenon; the opening and closing of the hood has been made as quick and easy as possible. After releasing the interior locks, a button on the centre console is pushed, and the hood mechanism unfolds automatically. The procedure is reversed when the hood is raised. A protective cover can be secured over the hood in the down position

Left

The Porsche 968 Cabriolet is not just a cut-down Coupé. It is a properly constructed and finished version built by ASC in Heilbronn, half an hour's drive north up the motorway from Zuffenhausen. Painting and major construction takes place at the Porsche factory, and the cabriolets are then returned to ASC for finishing specific to it – the rear seats and rear interior trim, electrically-powered hood and vibration dampers

Above
The hood material is double lined for strength and protection from the elements; it is an exceptionally good fit, and although, as would be expected, the cabriolet is slightly noisier than the Coupé, it does not reach an unacceptable level

Right
Not to be outdone in the good-weather-motoring stakes, the Coupé can be supplied with a detachable roof panel. The panel is unlocked with a handle and can then, by means of a centre console switch, either be tilted for ventilation, or removed entirely and stowed in the boot

Above
The boot is large enough for an average load, although there is a highish sill to be overcome. Split rear seats fold flat individually for increased luggage space

Right
The Coupé's rear hatch can be released electronically from within the car. It opens with ease, thanks to hydraulic struts. The fabric luggage cover lifts with it, but can be detached

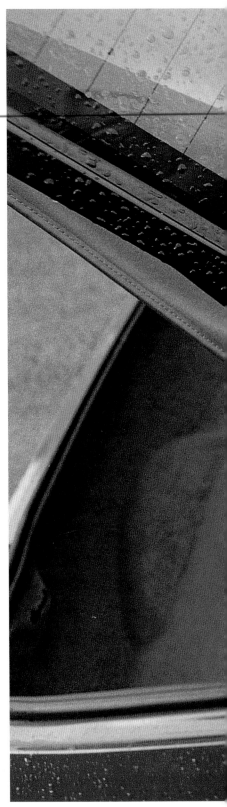

Above

Driver and front seat passenger travel in comfort. There is ample legroom, and the pedals are agreeably set. The seats are firmly comfortable rather than squashily so; they are electronically adjustable for a wide range of position combinations. As well as adding to comfort this makes getting in and out, particularly of the driving seat, a lot easier, although a memory setting would be particularly useful

Left

The rear seats themselves are small. Although adequate for medium sized children, they can only be used by larger ones or adults for short distances, and not at all by anyone over six feet tall, whatever their age. Porsche do supply a child safety seat especially designed for their range. All in all, the 968 can be described as a family car; it just depends what you mean by family!

Both Coupé and Cabriolet have efficient heating and ventilation systems, with a special control to ensure that no fumes can get into the car; unfortunately there is no guarantee that the outside air will always be as clean and pleasant as that found in the vineyards of Swabia

Zuffenhausen

In 1950, the 356 when went into serious production, it was built in the Zuffenhausen district of Stuttgart. The first cars bearing the Porsche name were created in an area just 90 feet square in the Reuter body works, while the original factory was occupied by the Americans. The optimistic production forecast was for around 500 cars for the world market in the first year. A year later Ferdinand Porsche died, but Zuffenhausen carried on to become a modern, automated, production line, now producing some 30,000 cars per annum. The company he created has become the largest manufacturer of specialised high performance cars in the world.

In order to keep up production 968 bodyshells are made independently, those for Coupés at Karmann and those for Cabriolets at ASC. They arrive at Zuffenhausen by rail where final assembly takes place after they are thoroughly inspected before beginning their transformation. Before it is ready for the road the 968 goes through sixteen workstations while, the chassis is assembled at twenty-four workstations.

Before painting can take place the bodies are secured to a mobile frame and cleaned, degreased and rinsed. The body is then given a coat of zinc phosphate, rinsed, passivated and rinsed again. A cathode bath primer coat is followed by more rinsing, then a robot-applied undercoat. The polyurethane-based filler coat which follows provides extra protection against stone chips. All the seams on the bodyshell are then sealed, and it is masked up ready for the undersealing. Made good and cleaned, it is now dried and cooled.

Porsche are rightly proud of their paint finish, indeed the entire bodywork construction; so much so that they offer a three year paintwork and ten year anti-corrosion warranty. before that paint is applied one task has to be performed that needs the human touch which automation cannot yet supply. The fine polishing which prepares the surface for its paint coats falls to human professionals. Human craftsmen also finish the door panels, dashboards and trim ready to be fitted once the painting process is completed.

'At Porsche, we only build sports cars.' Ferdinand Alexander Porsche in his introduction to the 968 selling brochure sums up the company philosophy

When the body comes to be painted there is a choice of nearly 200 colours, amongst which mint Green and Rubystone Red rank as the most novel. The cars are painted relatively close to each other, whatever the colour each might be, with the overspray isucked downwards and out of harm's way by a system which also cuts down on the noxious substances released into the atmosphere.

Once the matt black parts have been sprayed, the hollow panels are protected with sealant, and the shells head for the assembly line where the chassis number is engraved by laser.

Meanwhile, the chassis takes shape heat exchanger, fuel and brake lines, petrol tank, engine, propeller shaft, gearbox, windscreen, console, steering wheel, steering box, wheel housings, bumpers, rear seats, exhaust, electrics, cooling and braking systems are all installed.

Finally the bodyshell and chassis are put together and finishing takes place. The wheels and front seats are fitted; oil, petrol and windscreen cleaner are added.

At this point, cabriolets are taken back to ASC where the parts specific to this car are fitted as part of the final finish; the rear seats, rear interior trim, electrically-powered hood, door trims and vibration dampers.

Above

The body is now ready for a coat of zinc phosphate, rinsing, passivating and rinsing again. A cathode bath primer coat is followed by more rinsing, then a robot-applied undercoat. The polyurethane-based filler coat which follows provides extra protection against stone chips

Above right

All the seams on the bodyshell are now sealed, and it is masked up ready for the undersealing, one of the operations carried out by robots. Made good and cleaned, the bodyshell is now dried and cooled

Right

One of the most amazing sights at Zuffenhausen is the painting of several cars at once, in different colours, and in close proximity to each other. Overspray is sucked downwards and out of harm's way by a system which also has the environmental advantage of reducing CFC emissions

Up to two hundred special colours are available in addition to the standard range which has been expanded of late to incorporate some more unusual colours. Rubystone red and Mint green certainly turn a few heads. Paint inspections, which take place throughout the process are critical; any substandard finish must be spotted and dealt with immediately

Porsche naturally value their quality control procedures so these cars still come under the aegis of Porsche quality control staff. All 968s under thorough testing follows, including a stint on a rolling road.

Cars for the foriegn (ie not German) market are sprayed with protective wax ready for the journey, while German customers test drive the car, making sure it is completely satisfactory.

Above
Another area where there is no substitute for the handiwork of a craftsman; door panels, dashboards and trim are expertly finished by hand ready for fitting

Right
Once the matt black parts have been sprayed, the hollow panels are protected with sealant, and the shells head for the assembly line. During the assembly process the bodyshells are placed on an assembly frame, which is automatically steered to the production line. All the masking from the paintshop is removed, and many of the bodypanels are protected by covers

The chassis number is engraved by laser; the transformation of the bodyshell into a 968 will soon be complete

Above
Once positioned correctly, the glass panels are secured with tape; the adhesive will cure while the car continues down the production line

Left
Glass is fixed in place with a combined adhesive sealant that owes its development to space technology

Above

Bodyshell and chassis are now married up by means of a suspended frame, and finishing can take place. The wheels and front seats are fitted; oil, petrol and windscreen cleaner are added

Right

The car will pass through sixteen workstations on its journey; braking system, pedals, cables, heating and air conditioning, dashboard, door trims, carpets, soundproofing, steering rack and boot. A thorough inspection follows. Meanwhile, the chassis will be being assembled at twenty-four different workstations; heat exchanger, fuel and brake lines, petrol tank, engine, propeller shaft, gearbox, windscreen, console, steering wheel, steering box, wheel housings, bumpers, rear seats, exhaust, electrics, cooling and braking systems; and of course another inspection

Above

Cars that are to be shipped are sprayed with protective wax ready for the journey. Customers from Germany are then invited to test drive the car, making sure it is completely satisfactory. A final inspection and cleaning, and the car can be collected. Another 968 is ready for the road

Right

At this point, cabriolets are taken back to ASC for finishing. They fit the parts specific to this car, the rear seats, rear interior trim, electrically-powered hood, door trims and vibration dampers. Quality control is still the responsibility of Porsche quality control staff. Thorough testing follows; the quality control unit inspects every aspect of the car, and it is put through its paces on a rolling road. Steering geometry and headlight beams are set up

Opposite

All-weather performance of a different kind. The Cabriolet's hood in both the up and down positions, a transformation that takes place at the push of a button

Above

The sun is shining and the hood is down. A 968 Cabriolet is ready to hit the road

The Test

On 22nd January 1992, a very special endurance test began at the Weissach Development Centre. The intention was to to take a 968 across three continents and allow the car to experience extreme driving conditions that would push it to the limits. The test aim was to cover 100,000 kilometers in 100 days; but this was to be no mad dash for a goal for its own sake. The marathon drive was carefully planned to incorporate terrain and conditions that would equate the run to five car life-cycles in terms of the demands made on it. The 968 used was a standard production model with the Tiptronic gearbox.

The driver chosen for the test was Gerhard Plattner. He already held the record for driving around the world – in twenty-eight days and sixteen hours – and would record his two-millionth kilometer during this journey.

There were six particular tests incorporated into the marathon, each of which were potentially fraught with problems.

One major milestone was the first drive of a catalytic-converter sports car through the desert in Morocco and across the Atlas mountains. Poor roads and the non-availability of unleaded fuel would previously have made such a trip unthinkable.

Less problematic was the economy run which took place between the most westerly and easterly capitals of the former Austro-Hungarian Empire, Innsbruck and Budapest. Just one tank of fuel was used, to prove that the 240 bhp 968 can be frugal, even though it has a top speed of more than 150 mph (250 km/h). The guest driver for this section was Karl Habsburg-Lothringen, appropriately the grandson of the last Austrian Emperor. Ninety years previously, the young Ferdinand Porsche had chauffeured a Habsburg Duke from a previous generation in his gasoline-electric Lohner-Porsche; by all accounts the Duke had been impressed.

The A7 is the longest autobahn in Germany at 578 miles (963 km) long. From Flensburg, near the Danish border, it heads south, through Hamburg, Hannover, Kassel and Wurzburg, beyond Ulm to the Austrian border. Plattner and his team drove along its length three times in 24 hours, naturally adhering to any speed restrictions. Including refuelling stops, this part of their journey represented an average speed of 72 mph (120 km/h).

The only disappointment of the adventure concerned the altitude test. A 24 hour drive over the 10 mile (17 km) road between the Sellajoch and

Gerhard Plattner (left) with members of his team and the car that covered 100,000Km in under 100 days

Grodnerjoch mountain passes, which would have resulted in a 31 mile (56 km) total change in altitude over the time, had to be abandoned, but not because of the cars' capabilities – the passes had been closed due to the imminent danger of avalanche.

The next phase took place in North America. The first test was a drive across the ice, from Inuvik to Tuktoyaktuk, 120 miles (200 km) further north, on the Mackenzie bay. This Eskimo settlement can only be reached by 'land' – by ice in fact, between December and April, when the temperature of minus 37° Celsius ensures a firm base, if a slippery surface. After a journey down the Alaska Highway and across Yellowstone Park, there followed the second part of the American leg; several hours spent on the famous Bonneville Salt Flats race track. This part of the journey ended at the most southerly point of the US – Key West in Florida, where the temperature measured 26° Celsius. The 63° change

over 110 hours did not affect the car, although one suspects the occupants cheered up enormously once they got to Florida!

For the last part of the test, it was necessary to abandon public roads, sand tracks and ice rinks, for a purpose-built location, the Nardo test track in Italy. Having already covered 90,000 of the toughest kilometers, the car proved that it could perform just as efficiently on a track, covering 5566 kilometers in 24 hours at full throttle, stopping only for fuel and a brief visual check. Average speeds were more than 130 mph (220 km/h). Following its performance at Nardo, the 968 exhaust was tested; emissions were virtually unchanged – and well below the legal limit.

The car continued on the last section of its run; 100,000 km was recorded three days sooner than had been anticipated. The journey finished at a television studio in Cologne; there had been no technical faults or defects, no problems or stresses with the car. The only repair

Above and right
Equally at home on the wide expanse afforded by a beach or on narrow cobbled roads, the 968 turns heads wherever it goes

Right

Porsche sporting history began with a victory at Le Mans in 1951 for two Frenchmen, Veuillet and Mouche, in a 356. Between 1976 and 1977 the 935 won the World Endurance Championship for Makes for Porsche. Changes in group 5 racing regulations gave the car an aerodynamically improved body, with consequent reduction in air resistance. This was the most powerful version of the six-cylinder engine so far; for the first time in Porsche's history, it was fitted with water-cooled cylinder heads with four valves per cylinder – the cylinders themselves remained air-cooled. The car was nicknamed 'Moby Dick'

Above

The 935 is one of the many cars from Porsche's history which can be seen in their Museum in Zuffenhausen, just across the road from the main factory building. The museum is open to the public; as well as racing and production cars, there is also an audio-visual theatre with multi-language presentations

during the whole trip was of a broken tank lid.

The car was returned to the Weissach centre, where it was stripped down and inspected in the minutest of detail. There were no parts that needed replacement, no abnormal wear to indicate the marathon which had just taken place. Sand, ice, extremes of temperature and weather conditions had been experienced, and valuable lessons were learned by the Weissach experts; the invaluable knowledge they gained help both in the continuous improvement of current models and the development of new ones.

'Car and Driver' – lamenting the fact
that their 968 failed to reach the States
in time for a four way sports car test
they had arranged – were impressed.
'Your memory will long retain the
sensations you absorb at the wheel. That
makes the 968 rare, even among
memorable competitors.'

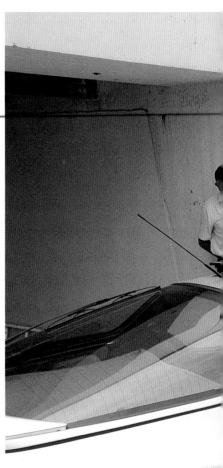

Above

'...Its slotted nose, laid-back headlights, and furl of wing...show that Porsche lifted its functional character cues off everything from its 959 supercar to today's 911 derivative Carrera models, to the bigger 928. They all mirror Porsche's image.'

Right

'People walk up to the 968 as if trying to place a face...'

Above

A few months later, having driven the 968 in cabriolet form, the 'Car and Driver' tester was happy to report that it felt as substantial with hood up or down, and felt as confident probing its limits as he had done with the Coupé version

Left

The Porsche repays being driven well. To this end, the company offer their customers the opportunity of attending the Porsche Driving School. These two day courses are usually held either at the Nürburgring or the Hockenheim Formula One circuit

Above

The aim of these courses is not to teach performance driving but to give drivers the opportunity of improving and practising both basic and more advanced driving skills – thus adding to both the pleasure and safety of motoring

Right

Within three-quarters of an hour of leaving the Porsche complex at Stuttgart, it is possible to be driving through the beautiful vineyard covered hills of one of Germany's top wine growing regions. The views are exceptional, the roads wind through the hills and the hairpin bends are spectacular

It isn't only at the Weissach proving ground that Porsche test of course; the severity factor is very different at, say, the North loop of Germany's Nurburgring and the high-speed track at Nardo, Italy. Cobblestones should be all in a day's work. A very upmarket burger joint backdrop: fast food, fast car

Above

There is immense satisfaction in mastering the technique of approach and acceleration away from bends. In gentle mode, the torque shows, but the fun is to forget the torque, keep the revs up and revel in the limpet-like hold on the road

Right

Equally impressive is the 968's ability to eat up the miles – Autobahn – Autoroute – Motorway – Freeway. The test facilities at Weissach that produce a car like this are awesome: everything from variable-parameter engine endurance test rigs to a high-altitude climatic simulation chamber. 40 stylists and about 1,500 engineers and designers strive for this kind of result

Above
Porsche quote a driver of the nineteen fifties describing the daily use of his car as
'driving in its finest form.' Forty years later, they intend that these words should still
apply. The daily use of a Porsche should still be a pleasure, even though traffic has
increased and restrictions have multiplied

Right
Driving in its finest form, say Porsche, is driving in the most responsible manner. Using
the smallest possible area of road, with the lowest possible consumption, and doing the
least environmental damage

... And finally

Right

What of the future? A Club Sport version of 968 was introduced at the Paris motor show in September 1992. It is 50 Kg lighter than the standard car. The seats are adjusted and the windows opened manually while the level of trim has been reduced. This version is fitted with Recaro seats and the suspension has been lowered by 20mm. It comes with the six-speed manual gearbox

Overleaf

It is probable that 1993 will bring a new shape for 911. It is likely to have much in common looks-wise with 968 (at the front at least)

Above

And 928? There are rumours that it is nearing the end of its innings (in its present form at least), but the rumours have been around for nearly as long as the car itself

Left

Meanwhile, 968 will continue to represent Porsche at the less expensive end of its car range with five options; Coupé or Cabriolet with manual gearbox or Tiptronic, and the manual Club Sport

Above
'…what is important is to do them well.' In terms of drivability, construction and finish, safety, economy and sheer motoring enjoyment this is what the world famous badge from Zuffenhausen has come to represent

Right
The lines of the 968 lend themselves extremely well to open-top style, arguably true of all Porsche creations

1. Retractable headlamps, with variable focal point reflector system to increase the light output. Additional driving lamp and when required front foglamps.

2. Inline, 16-valve, water-cooled, 3-litre, 4-cylinder engine. DME digital fuel injection and ignition with Electronic Octane ™ Knock Control. 240 bhp (DIN) at 6200 rpm. Top speed of 156 mph (252 km/h), 0-62.5 in 6.5 seconds.

3. Fully galvanised, steel construction, (with 2-year mechanical, 3-year paintwork and 10-year anti-corrosion body warranties).

4. Impact absorbing front section with integrated radiator and brake cooling inlets.

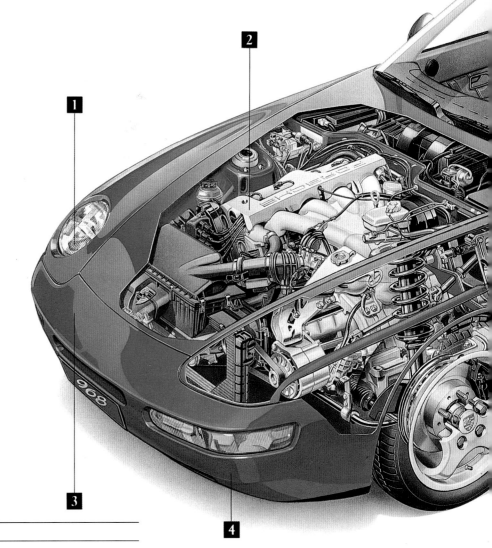

Technical Data

Engine

Number of cylinders	4	Maximum power – kW (bhp DIN)/at rpm	176 (240)/6200
Bore (mm)	104	Maximum Torque – Nm (EEC kpm)/at rpm	305 (31.5)/4100
Stroke (mm)	88	Output per litre – kW (bhp DIN)	58.9 (80.3)
Capacity cm^3 (effective)	2990	Petrol octane rating (RON)	98 unleaded (Super plus)
Compression ratio	11.0:1		

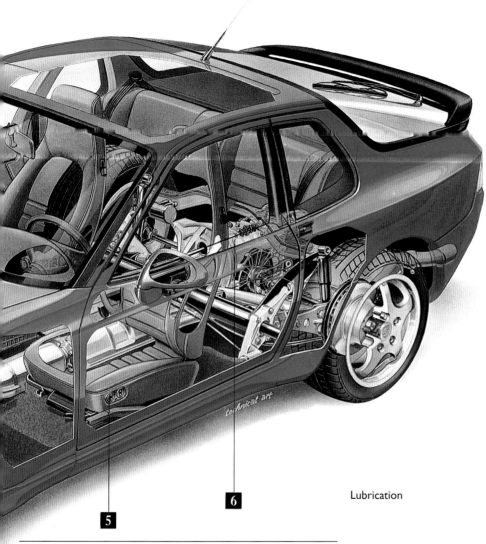

5. 2+2 seating with electrical height adjustment, available in fabric, leatherette and leather combinations.

6. Rear-mounted transmission connected to the engine via a transaxle tube. Rear wheels individually suspended on light alloy semi-trailing arms and transversed torsion bars.

Engine Design

Type and layout	Front-mounted, water-cooled inline, light alloy 4-cylinder, four-stroke with 2 contra-rotating balancer shafts (equipped with 3 way metallic exhaust gas catalytic converter).
Valve arrangement per cylinder	2 inlet, 2 exhaust, V formation overhead valves
Valve operation	Double overhead camshafts, self-adjusting hydraulic cam followers. VarioCam camshaft timing.

Lubrication	Forced feed lubrication, thermostatically controlled oil cooler, full flow filter.
Fuel injection	DME Digital Motor Electronics with self adaption, diagnosis, deceleration fuel cut off and idle stabilisation.

Electrical system

Battery (V)	12
Battery capacity (AH)	63
Alternator	115 A/1610 W
Ignition	Digital Motor Electronics control (DME) and 'Electronic Octane™TM Knock Control'

Transmission

Basic concept	Transaxle driveline connectin front mounted engine to rear mounted gearbox.
Manual gearbox	Full synchromesh with six forward and one reverse gears, with double mass flywheel.
Tiptronic dual function transmission	Four forward and one reverse gears, parking position, manual and automatic gear selection.

Body

Type	2-door, 2 + 2 Coupé and Cabriolet; constructed from hotdipped, cold rolled zinc dipped fully galvanised steel and polyurethane panels.

Chassis and Suspension

Front suspension	Fully independent with light wishbones and McPherson struts; coil springs enclosing telescopic dampers; anti-roll bars.
Rear suspension	Fully independent with light alloy semi-trailing arms and reinforced transverse torsion bar suspension, incorporating torsion bar for each wheel in transverse axle tube; telescopic dampers; anti roll bars.
Shock absorbers/Braking system	Double acting, gas pressure front and hydraulic rear Anti-lock braking system (ABS); dual circuit, servo-assisted hydraulic system; internally ventilated front and rear discs equipped with 4 piston aluminium fixed brake calipers; pressure compensating valve for the rear braking circuit; forced air cooling for front brake discs; asbestos-free brake pads; brake pad wear indicator; handbrake acting mechanically on rear wheel.

Right
New kid on the block for 1993: the Club Sport. Manual transmission for those who love to drive

Wheels	Pressure cast light alloy Cup Desig wheels with 7 J x 16 front; 8 J x 16 rear.
Tyres	205/55 ZR 16 front; 225/50 ZR 16 rear
Steering	Rack and pinion steering with collapsible steering column; progressive power assistance.

Dimensions

Wheelbase	2400 mm
Track, front	1472 mm
Track, rear	1450 mm
Overall length	4320 mm
Overall width	1735 mm
Helght (unladen)	1275 mm
Ground clearance (laden)	125 mm
Turning circle	10.75 m

Weights

Unladen weight (DIN standard)	Coupé 1370 kg [1400 kg] Cabriolet 1440 kg [1470 kg]
Maximum permitted weight	Coupé 1700 kg [1730 kg] Cabriolet: 1760 kg [1790 kg]

Performance

Maximum speed mph (kh/h)	156 mph (252 km/h) [153 mph (247 km/h)]
Acceleration 0-62.5 mph (0-100 km/h)	Coupé 6.5 secs [7.9 secs] Cabriolet 6.6 secs [8.3 secs]
Fuel consumption	
Constant speed 56 mph (90 km/h)	39.3 mpg (7.2 l/100 km) [39.8 mpg (7.1 l/100 km)]
Constant speed 75 mph (120 km/h)	32.08 mpg (8.8 l/100 km) [32.45 mpg (8.7 l/100 km)]
Urban cycle	19.08 mpg (14.8 l/100 km) [19.34 mpg (14.6 l/100 km)]

Right

As with the exterior colour, a wide range of interior trim is available. As well as the standard colours and finishes, individual tastes and preferences are catered to. Whether the seats are finished in leather, cloth or leatherette, it is done to an extremely high standard, with attention to detail evident in the quality of all the stitching and piping

Standard Equipment for the 968

Much of the 968 standard equipment is just that, standard; you'll find similar items on a Vauxhall Nova. That's not to say that some of the equipment isn't special; deformable front and rear panels, seatbelt pre-tensioners, anti-roll bars, side intrusion bars and the brake system make for a real feeling of safety while the metallic exhaust gas catalytic converter is a definite plus in this 'green' age. I would question the need for heated door mirrors, but as Ferdinand Porsche said: '…what is important is to do them well.'

- Controlled 3-way metallic catalytic converter with Lambda sensor and closed fuel tank vent system
- 63 AH capacity battery
- 6-speed manual gearbox, with double mass fly wheel and two section clutch housing
- 16 in. pressure cast, light alloy 'Cup Design' wheels
- Lockable wheel nuts
- Dual circuit brake system with 4 internally ventilated discs, 4-piston aluminium fixed brake calipers
- Forced air cooled front brake discs
- Anti-lock braking system (ABS)
- Front and rear anti-roll bars
- Progressive power assisted steering
- Hot zinc-dipped fully galvanised bodywork
- Side instrusion bars fitted in the doors
- PVC underbody protection
- Cavity wax protection
- Underbody protection
- Laminated windscreen
- Tinted glass
- Roof mounted radio antenna (Cabriolets have amplified in-screen aerial)
- Deformable front polyurethane panel with integral light metal bumper
- Deformable rear polyurethane panel with mtegral light metal bumper
- Heated rear windscreen (Coupé only)
- Electrically operated hood with manual locking (Cabriolet only)
- Rear spoiler (Coupé only)
- Retractable main headlamps
- Internally adjustable headlamp beams
- Additional parking lamps
- Multi-focus foglamps
- Rear fog lamp
- High intensity rear lamps
- Electrically adjustable, heated door mirrors
- Heated windscreen washers
- 3-speed windscreen wipers
- Variable intermittent wipe facility
- Rear window wiper (Coupé only)
- Integrated central locking and alarm, key operated with flashing LEDs incorporated into the door lock buttons. Includes automatic ignition and fuel cut-outs
- 6-speaker sound system
- Cassette and coin holder
- Electrically operated windows
- Four spoke leather covered steering wheel
- Leather covered gear lever and hand-brake lever
- Vanity mirror with sliding safety cover on driver and passenger sun visors (Coupé only)
- Front seats with electrical height adjustment
- Individually folding rear seats
- Front seat fitted with three-point inertia seat belt buckle on the seat base
- Rear seats fitted with three point inertia seat belts. (Cabriolet fitted with two point lap belts)
- Analogue clock
- Outside ambient temperature gauge
- Brake pad wear indicator
- Tachometer
- Oil pressure and oil level indicators
- Automatic heating control
- Four stage blower with air circulation system and defrost control
- Electrically operated luggage compartment release
- Rear luggage compartment cover (Coupé only)
- Automatic interior lamps with time delay
- Boot and engine lamps

As with most cars there is optional equipment available, again much of it fairly standard. Among the more interesting options are the limited slip differential (40 per cent locking factor), Tempostat Automatic Speed Control and, for the real speed freak, the full Sports chassis with 17 in. Pressure cast light alloy 'Cup Design' wheels.